MACLEO

MACLEOD

HOLD · FAST

Lewis tartan, Ardvreck Castle & plant badge, Red Whortleberry

CLAN
MACLEOD

Extensively Revised

COMPILED BY
Alan McNie

CASCADE PUBLISHING COMPANY
Jedburgh, Scotland

Genealogical Research:
Research regrettably cannot be undertaken by the publisher. A non-profit organisation, The Scots Ancestry Research Society, 3 Albany Street, Edinburgh, undertake research for an agreed fee.

ISBN 0 9076144 5 0

Page 1 Explanation:
The illustrated tartan is the modern Macleod of Harris. In the artist's montage the present clan seat, Dunvegan Castle, depicted and in the foreground is the Harris plant badge, the Juniper.

MacLeod Country
DETAIL MAP OVERLEAF

The map used below and on the following page is intended basically as a pictorial reference. It is accurate enough, however, to be correlated with a current map. The clan boundaries are only marginally correct. No precise boundaries were kept in early times and territories were fluctuating frequently.

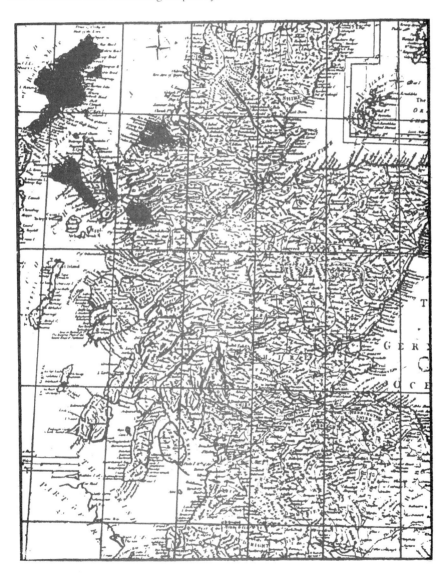

MacLeod
CLAN MAP

1. Ardvreck Castle, Loch Assynt Macleod of Lewis seat, now in ruins

2. Boreraig, nr. Dunvegan Head Home of piping MacCrimmons, hereditary pipers to MacLeod of MacLeod

3. Brochel Castle, Raasay Ruined island home of MacLeods of Raasay

4. Dunvegan Castle Clan seat with parts dating from 15th century

5. Glenelg Likely earliest MacLeod possession and commemorative black bull in clan crest originated here

6. Iona Seven MacLeod chieftains buried here

7. Kilmuir Churchyard, Dunvegan Burial place of last five chiefs of MacLeod

8. Lews Castle, Stornoway Stronghold of MacLeods of Lewis, now in ruins

9. Rodel Church, Harris Contains some notable MacLeod tombs

10. Trumpan Church congregation of Vaternish massacred by MacDonalds

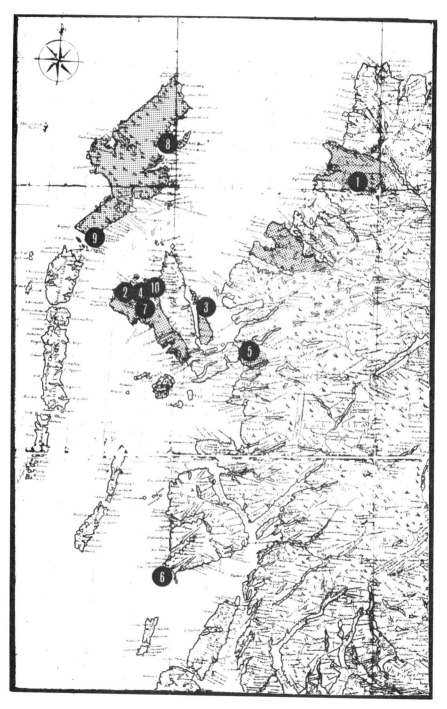

Dunvegan Castle

CLAN
MACLEOD

Condensed from Highland Clans of Scotland
George Eyre-Todd, 1923

Many hundreds of visitors to the Outer Hebrides today are familiar with the noble old towers of Dunvegan at the head of Loch Bracadale on the western side of Skye. The ancient seat of the MacLeods towering on its rocks is not only the most romantic dwelling in the Isles, but the oldest inhabited mansion in Scotland, having been one of the sea-eyries built by the Norse rovers in the ninth or tenth century, and continuously inhabited to the present day. Nothing more picturesque could well be imagined than its cluster of square towers and embattled walls rising above the wild crags of the shore, and there is nothing more interesting in the record of the Western Isles than the story of the chiefs of MacLeod who, for so many centuries, have made it their stronghold and home. Probably no better description of the castle is to be found than that given by Sir Walter Scott in his diary of the voyage he made in the yacht of the Lighthouse Commissioners in August, 1814. This runs as follows: "Wake under the Castle of Dunvegan in the Loch of Folliart. I had sent a card to the Laird of MacLeod in the morning, who came off before we were dressed, and carried us to his castle to breakfast. A part of Dunvegan is very old; 'its birth tradition notes not.' Another large tower was built by the same Alister MacLeod whose burial-place and monument we saw yesterday at Rodel. He had a Gaelic surname, signifying the Humpbacked. Roderick More (knighted by James VI) erected a long edifice combining these two ancient towers; and other pieces of building, forming a square, were accomplished at different times. The whole castle occupies a precipitous mass of rock overhanging the lake, divided by two or three islands in the place, which form a snug little harbour under the walls. There is a courtyard looking out upon the sea, protected by a battery — at least a succession of embrasures, for only two guns are pointed, and these unfit for service. The ancient entrance rose up a flight of steps cut in the rock, and passed into this courtyard through a portal, but this is now demolished. You land under the castle, and, walking round, find yourself in front of it. This was originally inaccessible, for a brook coming down on the one side, a chasm of the rocks on the other, and a ditch in front, made it impervious. But the late MacLeod built a bridge over the stream, and the present laird is executing an entrance suitable to the character of this remarkable fortalice, by making a portal between two advanced towers and an outer court, from which he proposes to throw a drawbridge over the the high rock in front of the castle. This, if well executed, cannot fail to have a good and characteristic effect."

On the first night of his visit Scott slept in the haunted chamber of the castle, which is still pointed out, and he gives an account of his impressions in the last of his "Letters on Demonology and Witchcraft." He had previously slept in the haunted chamber of the ancient castle of Glamis in Strathmore, and his impressions here were somewhat similar. "Amid such tales of ancient tradition," he says, "I had from MacLeod and his lady the courteous offer of the haunted apartment of the castle, about which, as a stranger, I might be supposed interested. Accordingly I took possession of it about the witching hour. Except, perhaps, some tapestry hangings, and the extreme thickness of the walls, which argued great antiquity, nothing could have been more comfortable than the interior of the apartment; but if you looked from the windows, the view was such as to correspond with the highest tone of superstition. An autumnal blast, sometimes clear, sometimes driving mist before it, swept along the troubled billows of the lake, which it occasionally concealed, and by fits disclosed. The waves rushed in wild disorder on the shore, and covered with foam the steep pile

Sir Walter Scott

of rocks, which, rising from the sea in forms something resembling the human figure, have obtained the name of Macleod's Maidens, and, in such a night, seemed no bad representative of the Norwegian goddesses, called Choosers of the Slain, or Riders of the Storm. There was something of the dignity of danger in the scene; for, on a platform beneath the windows, lay an ancient battery of cannon, which had sometimes been used against privateers even of late years. The distant scene was a view of that part of the Quillen mountains which are called, from their form, MacLeod's Dining-Tables. The voice of an angry cascade, termed the Nurse of Rorie Mhor, because that chief slept best in its vicinity, was heard from time to time mingling its notes with those of wind and wave. Such was the haunted room at Dunvegan."

Among the characteristic relics in the castle, which Scott saw, and which are still treasured there, were the drinking horn of Rorie Mhor, an ox's horn tipped with silver, which each chief of the MacLeods, on coming of age, was expected to drain at a single draught; the Dunvegan cup, a beautifully chased and ornamented silver chalice of the fifteenth century, which Scott by a misreading of the inscription round its rim made out to date from 500 years earlier; and the famous Fairy Flag said to have been given to a Chief of the MacLeods either by an Irish princess or a fairy bride, but which is most likely a trophy brought home from one of the crusades by some early warrior. "It is a pennon of silk with something like round red rough berries wrought upon it, and its properties," as, described by Scott, were that "produced in battle it multiplied the number of the MacLeods; spread on the nuptial bed it ensured fertility; and, lastly, it brought herring into the loch." According to tradition the flag has already been twice displayed, and produced its expected results. When displayed for the third time it will have the same effect, but it and its bearer will forthwith disappear from earth.

The Chief of MacLeod of Scott's time was busily engaged in planting trees and improving his estate. "If he does not hurry too fast," said the novelist, "he cannot fail to be of service to his people. He seems to think and act much like the chief, without the fanfaronade of the character." When Scott and his party left they were accompanied to the yacht by MacLeod himself, with his piper playing in the bows in proper style, and were sent off with a salute of seven guns from

Old Dunvegan Castle

Loch Assynt and Ardvreck Castle

the castle. The episode concludes with the entry, "the Chief returns ashore with his piper playing 'The MacLeods' Gathering,' heard to advantage along the calm and placid loch, and dying as it retreated from us."

Fifty years before Scott's time Dunvegan was visited by Dr Samuel Johnson and his biographer Boswell, both of whom have left characteristic records of their impressions paid by the poet Alexander Smith, who has left some account of it in his well-known book, *A Summer in Skye.* More recently still, a very full and excellent account of the castle and its chiefs is to be found in Canon MacCulloch's charming volume, *The Misty Isle of Skye.*

According to popular tradition, cited in Douglas's *Baronage,* the MacLeods were descended from the Norwegian kings of Man; but there is equally strong reason to believe that, in the male line at least, they belonged to the ancient Celtic inhabitants of the country. They come first out of the mists of the past as allodial owners of Glenelg, the possession of which was confirmed to them in the person of Malcolm, son of Tormod, by David II in the fourteenth century, in a charter under which the chief obliged himself to provide a galley of thirty-six oars for the king's use when required. Dunvegan and the lands of Skye came into MacLeod's possession by marriage with a daughter of MacRaild, the heiress of a Norwegian chief. At the same time, the MacLeod chiefs appear to have been owners of lands in Harris and the Lewis.

A younger brother of Tormod, already mentioned, Torquil MacLeod of the Lewis, married the heiress of the Chief of the MacNicols, and through her came into possession of the district of Assynt and other lands in Wester Ross, for which he obtained a charter from David II. His descendants became independent chiefs, and were known as the Siol Thorcuil or Race of Torquil, while the descendants of his elder brother were known as the Siol Thormod or Race of Tormod. At a later day the MacLeods of Assynt were represented by MacLeod of Raasa. These MacLeods of Lewis and Assynt had their own history, which was stirring enough. There is in particular the much-disputed episode of the arrest of the great Marquess of Montrose in 1651, which by some is held to have cast a stain upon the name, and by others is believed not to have been the work of MacLeod of Assynt at all, but of his wife or one of his clansmen in the ordinary course of duty in his absence.

Meanwhile the MacLeods of MacLeod, the race of Tormod, with their seat at Dunvegan, played a most notable part in the history of the Western Isles. They were among the chiefs who fought on the side of Bruce, and a son of the Chief accompanied Donald of the Isles in the raid which ended at the battle of Harlaw in 1411. A typical incident of that history was the feud with the MacKays, of which the most outstanding incident was a bloody battle on the marches of Ross and Sutherland in the first years of the fifteenth century, from which the only survivor on MacLeod's side was a solitary clansman who made his way, seriously wounded, home to his native Lewis, told his tale and died in the telling of it. Another famous feud was that which followed the marriage of MacLeod of the Lewis with the widow of the Chief of the Mathiesons of Lochalsh, executed by James I at Edinburgh in 1427. Disputes arose between MacLeod and his stepsons, the young Mathiesons, John, the elder of these, sought the protection of his maternal grandfather, Chief of the MacIntosh's, and by and by, with the help of the latter, returned to claim his possessions. He attacked the castle of Lochalsh in which MacLeod and his wife defended themselves. When the stronghold was set on fire Mathieson, anxious to save his mother, stationed himself at the gate, and gave orders that she was to be allowed to pass. When she did so in the darkness and tumult, it was not noticed that she was taking with her, hidden under the wide folds of her arisaid or belted plaid the person of her husband, MacLeod himself. Presently the latter returned with a force of his own men from the Lewis, but was repulsed by young Mathieson, chiefly by the help of his bowmen, from which fact the battle is still called Blar nan Saigheadear. Making still another attempt to recapture the castle, MacLeod was slain and the feud ended.

One of the great battles in which the MacLeods engaged with their enemies of the Isles is commemorated in the name of the Bloody Bay, on the coast of Mull, two miles north of Tobermory, where the Macdonalds, under Angus Og, son of the last Lord of the Isles, about 1484, overthrew the fleet of James III, fitted out by the earls of Atholl and Argyll, and MacLeod of Harris, was slain.

The MacLeods, however, were still to perform an act of friendship

Edinburgh Castle

Stornoway Castle

towards the MacDonalds. At the end of the fifteenth century, when James IV was endeavouring to put an end to the constant clan troubles in the Hebrides, caused by the efforts to revive the broken power of the Lord of the Isles, Torquil MacLeod of the Lewis was the most notable of the chiefs who resisted the efforts of the king's lieutenants, first the Earl of Argyll and afterwards the Earl of Huntly. It was only by the efforts of James IV himself that the Islesmen were finally brought to peaceful submission. Last of them all, Torquil MacLeod – who, by the way, was Argyll's brother-in-law, and had been forfieted by command of parliament – retired to his stronghold of Stornoway Castle. He had with him his relative, Donald Dubh, son of that Angus Og who had won the battle of the Bloody Bay, and claimant of the Lordship of the Isles. But in the end Stornoway Castle was captured by the Earl of Huntly, Donald Dubh driven to Ireland, and the insurrection of the Islesmen brought to an end.

Perhaps the most tragic incident connected with Dunvegan took place in the middle of the sixteenth century. In 1552 William, the ninth chief, died. In the absence of his two brothers, Donald and Torquil, the clansmen acknowledged as chief Ian the Fair-haired, a descendant of the sixth Chief of the MacLeods. On the return of Donald a meeting was held at Lyndale, when Ian the Fair-haired was again chosen chief. Donald thereupon retired to Kingsburgh. Here he was approached by Ian Dubh, a son of Ian the Fair-haired, with offers of friendship, and, being enticed to a meeting at midnight, was forthwith slain, with six of his followers. Ian the Fair-haired ordered the arrest of Ian Dubh, but died before it could be effected. His eldest son Tormod was dead, but had left three sons, to whom Donald Breac, the brother of Ian Dubh, was guardian. When Donald Breac and the three boys returned from the funeral they found Dunvegan in possession of Ian Dubh, with the boys' mother a prisoner within. On Donald demanding possession, the doorway at the top of the narrow stair above the landing-place opened, and Ian Dubh appeared in full armour. Donald rushed up to the attack but was presently slain. The three sons of Tormod were also put to the sword by Ian Dubh, who proceeded to shut up his remaining brothers, with the wives and children of the other leaders of the clan, in the castle dungeons.

The Campbells now stepped in as guardian of Mary, the only child of the ninth chief, William. They landed with a large force at Roag in Loch Bracadale, met Ian Dubh in the church of Kilmuir, and arranged terms. Ian Dubh then invited the eleven Campbell chieftains to a feast at Dunvegan. The feast is said to have taken place in what is now the drawing-room of the castle. There each Campbell found himself seated between two MacLeods. At the end of the feast, instead of a cup of wine, a cup of blood was set before each guest, and forthwith at the signal each Campbell was stabbed in the throat by a MacLeod.

The final scene in the drama took place in 1559. Torquil MacLeod, brother of the ninth Chief, then arrived to claim the chiefship, and a warder, Torquil MacSween, was induced to betray the castle. Hearing a noise, Ian Dubh sprang from bed. Seeing all was lost he fled to his galley and escaped to Harris. Thence he made his way to Ireland, where presently he was seized by the O'Donnell chief, and horribly slain by having a read-hot iron thrust through his bowels.

But the main feuds of the MacLeods were with the MacDonalds of the Isles, who were their own near neighbours in Skye. Already in the days of King Robert III they had signally defeated that powerful clan, but it was towards the close of the sixteenth century that the most notable events in the feud occurred. In the latter part of the century the MacLeans of Mull were at bitter feud with the MacDonalds of Islay. In that feud they were generously helped by the MacLeods. One of the traditions of Dunvegan of that time is told in *A Summer in Skye*. On a certain wild night MacDonald of Sleat was driven on his barge into the loch, and forced to ask shelter from MacLeod. He was admitted with his piper and twelve followers, but at dinner, noticing the ominous boar's head upon the table, refused to leave his men and sit above the salt. Over the wine after dinner some bad blood was occasioned by MacDonald's boasting about his dirk and his powers of using it, and a serious tragedy might have ocurred but for a sweetheart of one of the MacDonalds, who, as she passed her lover with a dish, whispered to him to beware of the barn in which he was to sleep. The man told his master, and, instead of going to sleep on the heaps of heather which had been prepared for them in the barn, the MacDonalds spent the night in a cave outside. At midnight the barn was a mass of flame, and the MacLeods thought they had killed

Flora Macdonald - near MacLeods of Skye

Loch Maree

their enemies; but presently, much to their astonishment they saw MacDonald march past the castle with his twelve men, his piper playing a defiance to Dunvegan, and, before anything could be done, the barge set sail and sped down the loch.

In the course of the warfare with the MacDonalds the most terrible event took place on the Isle of Eigg. The tradition runs that a small party of MacLeods had landed on that island, and ill-treated some of the women. They were seized, bound hand and foot, and set adrift in their own boat, but managed to reach Dunvegan. Forthwith, to avenge them, the MacLeod Chief sailed for Eigg. Seeing this overwhelming force the inhabitants of the island, some 200 in number, took shelter in a great cave which had a single narrow entrance. Their plan seemed successful. MacLeod searched the island, but failed to find them, and at last set sail. Looking back, however, the MacLeods spied a man on the top of the island. Returning immediately, by means of his footsteps in a sprinkling of snow which had fallen, they traced him to the mouth of the cave. There they demanded that the persons who had set their men adrift should be given up for punishment. This was refused; whereupon MacLeod ordered his men to gather heather and brushwood. This was piled against the mouth of the cave and set on fire. and the blaze was kept up until all within were suffocated to death.

By way of retaliation for this massacre, on a Sunday when the MacLeods of Vaternish were at service in the church at Trumpan, a body of MacDonalds from Uist, having landed at Ardmore, set fire to the fane, and burnt it with all its worshippers except one woman, who escaped through a window. The MacDonald galleys, however, and the smoke of the burning, had been seen from Dunvegan, and MacLeod had sent out the Fiery Cross. As he came within sight, the MacDonalds rushed to their boats; but the tide had left them high and dry, and as they struggled to launch them the MacLeods rushed to the attack, and everyone of the MacDonalds was slain. The bodies of the dead were laid in a long row beside a turf dyke at the spot, and the dyke was overthrown upon them, from which fact the battle is known as Blar Milleadh Garaidh, the Battle of the Spoiling of the Dyke. A few years later the MacDonalds made another raid and swept off all MacLeod's cattle; but they were overtaken near the same spot, a terrible fight took place, and nearly everyone of the MacDonalds was killed. It is said that on each side, on this last occasion, a blacksmith remained fighting in full armour. The MacLeod blacksmith was beginning to faint from loss of blood when his wife came upon the scene, and with a cry struck the enemy with her distaff. MacDonald turned his head, and at the moment was run through and slain. In the same battle a son of MacLeod of Unish was fighting valiantly when a MacDonald rushed at him, and hewed off his legs at the knees. Nevertheless, MacLeod continued to fight standing on his stumps, and the spot where at last he fell is still known after him as the Knoll of the Son of Ian.

Again, at Cnoc a Chrochaidh, the hanging-hill in the same neighbourhood, another act of justice took place. A son of Judge Morrison of the Lewis had been on a visit to Dunvegan, and afterwards on Asay island had killed some MacLeods. He was pursued and overtaken here, and hanged on three of his own oars. Before the hanging he was told to kneel and say his prayers, and long afterwards some silver coins found in a crevice of the rocks were believed to have been treasure concealed by him during his devotions.

It was at one of the battles near Trumpan that the fairy flag is believed to have been last displayed.

Perhaps most famous of the MacLeod chiefs was Roderick or Ruari More of Dunvegan, from whom the waterfall beside the castle takes its name. Along with his contemporary, Roderick MacLeod of the Lewis, he had resisted the order of King James VI that all landowners in the Highlands must produce their charters. Accordingly the property of the two chiefs was declared forfeited, and an attempt was made to settle Lewis and Skye by a syndicate from the East of Scotland. The Fife Adventurers reached the Western Isles late in 1598, but they were not long allowed to remain at peace. In the Lewis, Neil MacLeod rushed the settlement at dead of night and slew fifty of the colonists, and after a renewed attack and slaughter the rest were forced to depart home. A second attempt of the same kind was made in 1605, and a third in 1609, with the same disastrous consequences. Also in 1607 an attempt was made to form a contract with the Marquess of Huntly to effect the civilisation of Lewis and Skye by exterminating the inhabitants, and it only failed because the Privy Council would

Sheriffmuir battleground, where Macleods of Harris played prominent part

Bonnie Prince Charlie

not accept Huntly's offer of £400 Scots for the island. At the same time, Spens of Wormiston, who had received a grant of Dunvegan, was prevented by the MacLeod chief from obtaining possession, and at last in 1610 MacLeod was enabled to procure a free pardon, and was knighted by King James. It was this Chief who built Rorie More's Tower, and placed on it the effigies of himself and his lady, a daughter of Glengarry. He also added much to the family estates, and did his best to put an end to the ancient feuds with his neighbours.

In the Civil Wars the clan fought on the Royalist side, and at the battle of Worcester it suffered so severely that the other clans agreed it should not be asked to join any warlike expedition until its strength was restored. As a result of his loyalty, in 1655 MacLeod was fined £2,500, and obliged to give security to the amount of £6,000 sterling for his obedience to the Commonwealth.

The MacLeods were reported by General Wade in 1715 to be 1,000 strong; and in 1745 MacLeod, it was said, could put 900 men in the field. He did not, however, join Prince Charlie, though many of his clansmen fought on the Jacobite side.

A strange episode of that time, in which MacLeod was concerned, was the abduction of the unhappy Lady Grange. The lady's husband, a judge of the Court of Session, was a brother of the Jacobite Earl of Mar. The marriage was most unhappy, and the lady is said to have threatened to reveal her husband's Jacobite plots. Then in 1731 it was given out that Lady Grange had died, and there was a mock funeral in Edinburgh. Meanwhile, with the aid of the MacLeod Chief and Lord Lovat, she was carried off, kept first on the Isle of Heiskar, to the west of North Uist, and afterwards at the lonely St Kilda. In 1741 she managed to send letters to her law agent, Hope of Rankeillor, and the latter fitted out an armed vessel for her rescue. MacLeod, however, was forewarned, and had Lady Grange removed first to Harris and afterwards to Skye, where she wandered imbecile for some seven years. At last, in 1745, the year of Charles Edward's landing, she died. Another mock funeral then took place at Durinish, but she was really buried at Trumpan, where the Earl of Mar set up a monument to her memory a few years ago. Among the papers at Dunvegan are still extant the accounts of the unfortunate lady's board and funeral.

List of Emigrants assisted by the Highland and Island Emigration Society, and embarked on board the Ship *Araminta* which sailed from *Liverpool* for *Port Philip* on the *4th August* 1852

Number	Name	Age	Residence	Estate	Remarks
1.41	McLeod Torquil	24	Rassay	Mr Rainey	Ditto — Outfit provided by McRainy of Rassay.
	Margaret	27	"	"	
	Christy	28	"	"	
	Alexander	15	"	"	
	Ann	14	"	"	
	Neil	11	"	"	
	Catherine	7	"	"	
	Catherine	4	"	"	
1.51	MacKinnon Malcolm	49	Popmisdale	Strcabost	Po. Note £13.17.7½ strong healthy man. — N.B. The man & him & have off a daughter age 15 one adm 10 — behind
	James	40	"	"	
	Alex	7	"	"	
	Kenneth	2	"	"	
1.52	McRae, Malcolm	49	Ulis	Lord Macdonald	Received no aid — Dßriet Kaid G

MacLeod Associated Names

Associated names have a hazy history. Sometimes they had more than one origin; also clouding the precise location of a particular surname might be that name's proscription or of course a migrant population. Even the spelling of surnames was subject to great variations, shifting from usually Latin or Gaelic and heeding rarely to consistent spelling. In early records there can be several spellings of the same name. Undoubtedly contributing to this inconsistency is the handwriting in official records, which was often open to more than one spelling interpretation.

With regard to the 'Mac' prefix, this was, of course, from the Gaelic meaning, son of. It wasn't long before it was abbreviated to 'Mc' or 'M', until we have reached the position now where there are more 'Mc's' than 'Mac's'.

MACLEOD OF HARRIS

BEATON, BETHANE, BETON   The Skye Beatons, originated with the Beatons or Bethunes from Fife, who were descendants of the Lairds of Balfour. Dr Peter Bethune was a Skye settler in the 16th century. From his descendants have come many important Skye families. Other Beatons originated in Mull, with Maclean association.

GRIMMOND   This derived form of MacCrimmon, with its MacLeod of Harris associations, is a Perthshire surname. John Grimon, Perth witness, 1534. John Grimmond, Pitfour, Aberdeenshire (2M WN Mintlaw) resident, 1665. In 1698 William Gryman dwelt in Auchtergaves (Strathtay, Perthshire).

MACANDIE   Either a Highland name, Mac (Sh)anndai from the Lowland Scots, Sandy, or a small associated group from the MacLeod Harris island of Bernera, Sound of Harris. This sept in Gaelic, Clann Ic Anndaidh, from personal name on Old Norse of Andi. John McHandie, in 1580, was a tenant in Newmore, Ross-shire, (3M NNW Invergordon).

MACCRIMMON   From Gaelic MacCruimein, derived in turn from Old Norse, Hromund, famed protector. In 1595 Hector M'Crimmon, signed deed on behalf of Isabella, wife of Sir Rory Mor, who became a MacLeod of MacLeod chieftain. A MacCrimmon family became hereditary pipers to MacLeod of MacLeod, with the last in succession through to the first quarter 19th century. There is a monument to this unique family.

MACWILLIAM   From Gaelic MacUilleim, son of William, with descent from Wilean, son of Wallan, the fifth MacLeod chief. John M'Williame lived in Lochalsh 1548. Alexander McWilliam, inhabitant of Seaforth, 1721.

NORMAN   Anglicized form of Tormod. Siol Thormaid (race of Norman) is the early name of the MacLeods of Harris. Norman also from Old English, Noromann, a Dane. Normannus, Nicecomes, in 1128, was a Holyrood charter witness. John Normand, inquisition juror, Roxburgh, 1303. Norman also appears in 13th century Dumfriesshire.

WILLIAMSON   Son of William. In 1343, Adam, son of William, produced burgh accounts of Peebles to the Exchequer. John Willelmi, in 1434, was a Brechin official. Brothers, Jhone Williamson and Donald Willeam Allanson, acted as witness in Cawdor, 1527.

MACLEOD OF LEWIS

CALLAM, CALLUM   From surname of Glenbucket, Aberdeenshire family an abbreviation of Malcolm. Considered sept of MacLeod of Raasay. William Callum of Glenbucket fined for reset of proscribed MacGregors in Glenbucket, 1636.

MACAULAY   The Lewis MacAulays from Uig with name from Gunni Olafson expelled from Orkneys to Lewis where warmly welcomed. Lord MacAulay, the statesman and historian, was a Lewis MacAulay. MacAulay also originates from Irish personal name. Duncan M'Aninhlay, in 1581, was minister of Fortingall. John Makalley, Inverness resident, 1602. John Mackalla, Edinburgh armourer, 1684.

MACCALLUM   From Gaelic MacCaluim, son of the servant of Calum. Some MacCallums were adherents to the MacLeods of Raasay. Archibald M'Callome, Glassary minister, 1661 (4M NW Lochgilphead). Donald McCallum, witness at Poltalloch, Argyllshire (10M NW Lochgil).

MACNICOL, MACNICOLL.   From Gaelic M'Nicail, son of Nicol. Nicolas originally from Greek, conquering people. The MacNicols were formerly an independent clan with Ross-shire origins. They mostly moved to Skye when a chieftain's daughter married Torquil MacLeod of Lewis. MacNicoll of Portree, Skye formed one of the council of Macdonald of the Isles. Thomas Maknicoll, Glasgow witness, 1553.

MALCOLMSON   From son of Malcolm which sometimes was used as an anglicised form of MacCallum. Symon Malcomesson rendered homage in Berwickshire, 1296. Robert Malcolmson, Stirling burgess, 1437. Master Gilbert Malcolm was rector of Craignish, 1542.

NICHOL, NICHOLL, NICOL, NICOLL   Diminutive of personal name, Nicola or Nicholas, brought by Normans. The surname, victorious people, has Greek origins. George Nuckle became in 1671 deacon of Alyth. William Nuckle was an Aberdeen tailor, 1684.

NICHOLSON, NICOLSON   Son of Nicol. The Nicholsons from Skye have anglicised their name from Macnicol. William Nicholai, burgess of Glasgow, 1419-21. Gilbert Nicholai (Latin genetive) in 1435 was vicar of Alford. Patrick Nicholai was presbyter of Brechin, 1436.

NORRIE, NORRY   From Thomas Nory, an Aberdeenshire landowner, 1360. William Nory, St. Andrews cathedral canon, 1415. In 1433 William Nary leased Ladcassy in Angus.

TOLMIE   From local source. In the MacLeod-MacKenzie battle of 1611, John Tolmach was involved. Andrew Tolmi was burgh officer of Inverness, 1612-16. The Tolmies of Hebrides are listed Clann Talvaich.

The McIan illustration of MacLeod as published (mid-19th century) in 'The Clans of the Scottish Highlands'

Clan background excerpts from book referred to on facing page

The Armorial Bearings of MacLeod are azure, a castle, triple towered and embattled argent, masoned sable, port and windows, gules. Crest, a bull's head, cabossed sable, between two flags, gules, staves of the first. Motto, "Hold fast."

The Suaicheantas, fixed in the right side of the bonnet, is craohb Aiteann, Juniper bush, *Juniperis communis*.

Many piobaireachds were composed in commemoration of the battles, and other transactions, in which this clan were engaged, events which offered favourable opportunities for the exercise of the musical abilities of the MacCruimins, hereditary pipers to MacLeod. These pieces of music are a species of historical record; and some of them refer to circumstances which took place many centuries ago. In a list before us, besides the Salute to the chief, and Lament played at his funeral, which were transferrable from generation to generation, there are eight other pieces, most of which, with historic notes, are given in the publication for Her Majesty's Piper.

Nor was this clan deficient in members of poetical ability. Mairi Mighean Alasdair ruaidh, or Mary, daughter of Alexander the red, a relation of the chief, is the most celebrated composer of poetry in the Isles; and as it is believed she could neither read nor write, she affords a striking instance of the natural gift of poesy. Her style is quite original; and some of her modes of versification have neither been attempted by any one previous, nor since her time. She was born in 1569, and died at the age of 105; and she is described as wearing the tonnag, a sort of shawl, which is given in the female representative of the MacNicols, fastened with a large ornamental silver brooch; and she, latterly used a silver-headed cane. There was another daughter of a red Alexander, who likewise wooed the muses, but her name was Fionaghal, or the Fair Stranger — a name translated Flora, with as much propriety as if it had been made Fortuna!

The figure which illustrates this clan is clad in the dress usually worn when not fully armed for war. This plaid was a most useful vestment in so watery a climate as Skye; nor was it less necessary for the highlanders, who, in a thinly-peopled country, might, on occasion of sudden tempests, be storm-staid on desolated isles: in such cases it would enable them to bivouac in sufficient comfort.

It has previously been observed that, after the repeal of the act which proscribed the highland dress, considerable difficulty occurred in many instances, to determine the almost forgotten patterns of clan tartan, so long an illegal manufacture and material for dress.

Some Clan Notables

McLeod, Alexander *(1774 – 1833)* was the son of a Hebridean minister. Before he was seven he had mastered his Latin grammar. Shortly after emigration to America he was licenced to preach. He became one of the nation's foremost pulpit orators and was instrumental in forbidding communicant membership to slave holders.

MacLeod, John *(1782 – 1820)* A native of Dumbartonshire, he entered the navy as a surgeon and accompanied the embassy to China. On his return he published a book on his China travels.

MacLeod, Norman D. D. *(1783 – 1862)* Son of a Scottish manse he eventually became moderator of the General Assembly of the Church of Scotland. He is remembered for promoting education in the Highlands and engaging in charity work among his countrymen. A son of the same name also had an outstanding ministry.

McLeod, John *(1788 – 1849)* was a native of Stornoway. He entered the service of the Hudson's Company and in 1814 he was in charge of the post at Red River. His diary describing his defence of the post against the Nor'Westers was printed in 1908. He played a prominent part in the Selkirk trouble and in 1821 was chief trader.

Macleod, William *(1850 – 1929)* was born in London of a Highland father. He showed early promise as an outstanding and versatile Australian artist in stained glass, drawing and portraiture. He also contributed to the Bulletin where he subsequently became business manager and majority shareholder.

Macleod, John *(1876 – 1935)* This famous son of a Scottish manse was educated at Aberdeen University where he graduated in medicine with great distinction. He is best remembered for his work on carbohydrate metabolism, which led in conjunction with the work of others to the discovery of insulin, for which he was co-recipient of the Nobel Prize in 1923 with Frederick G. Banting.